TINY CACTUS PUBLISHING

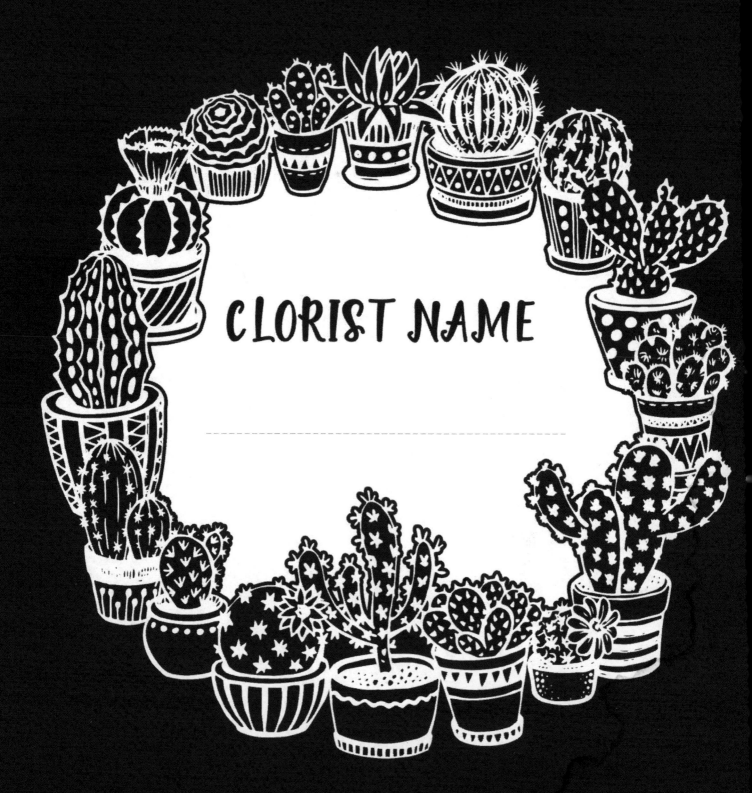

CLORIST NAME

TEST PAGE
PREPARE YOUR COLOR

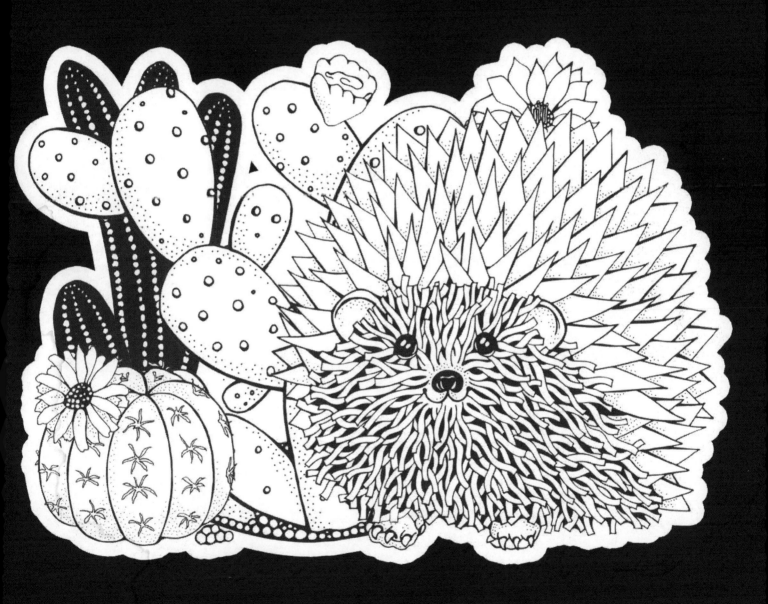

WARM UP !!

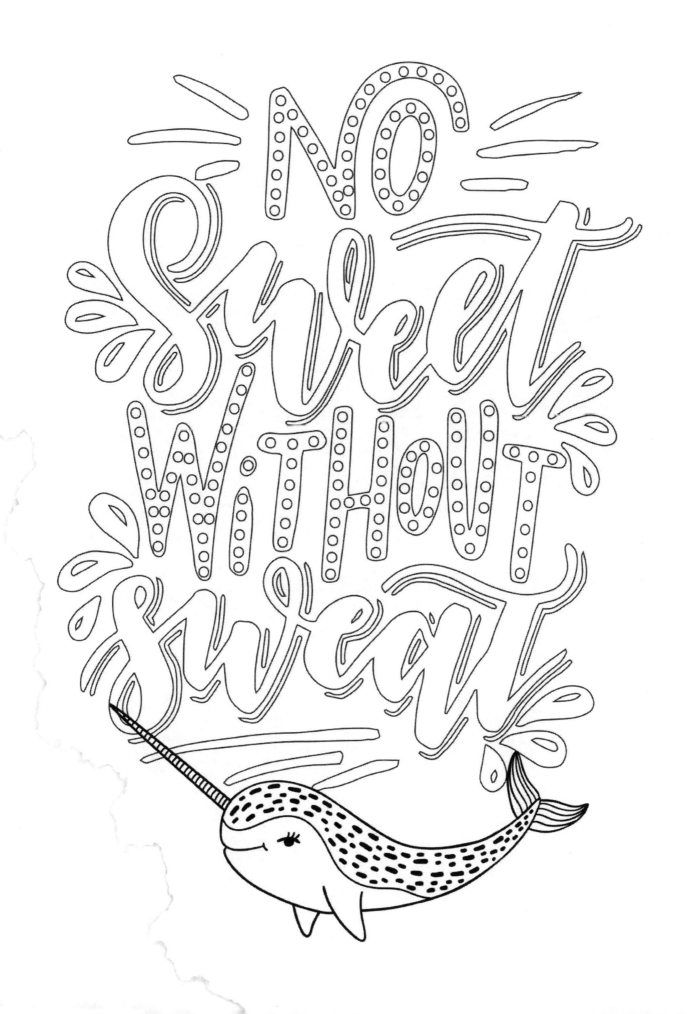

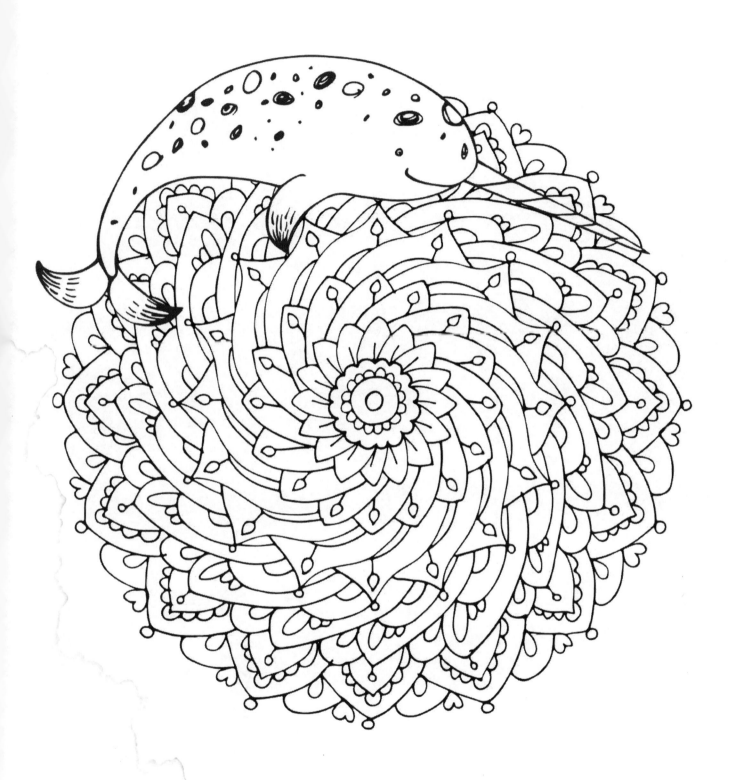

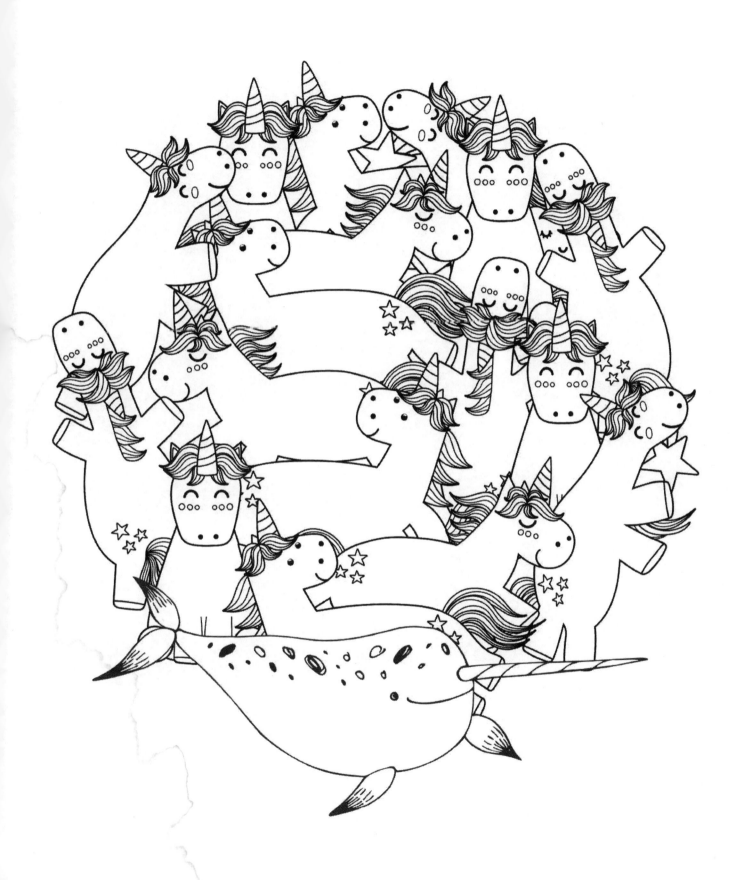

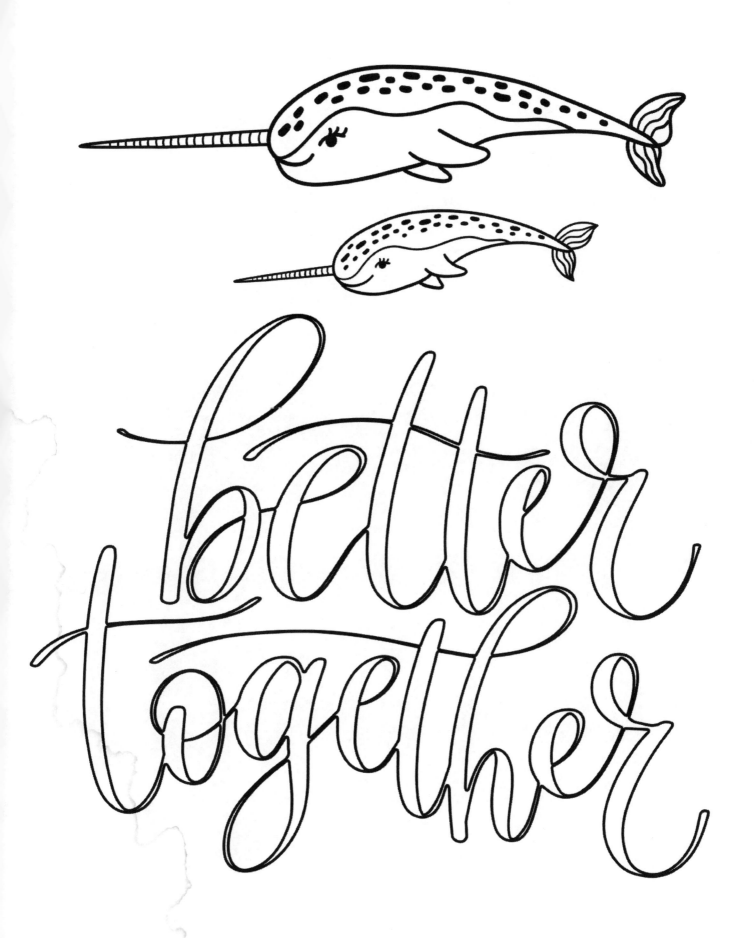

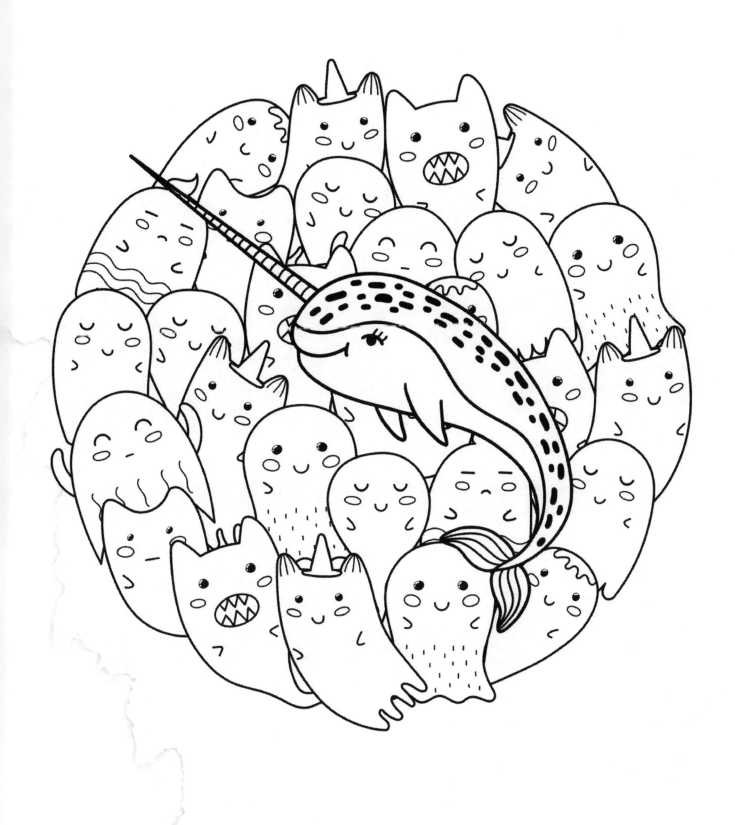

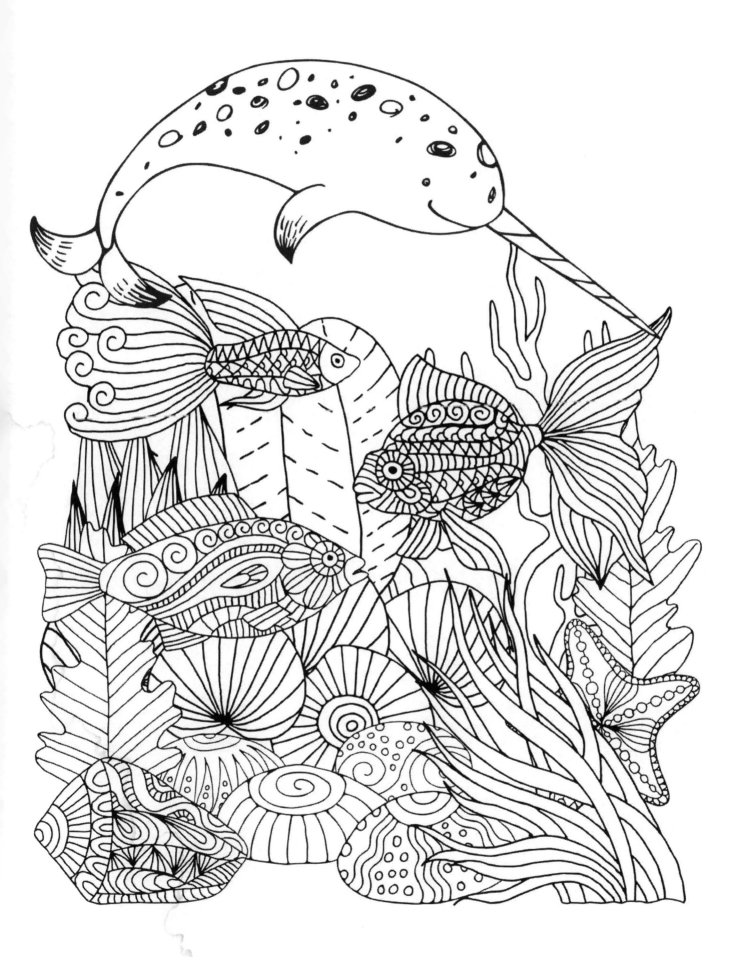

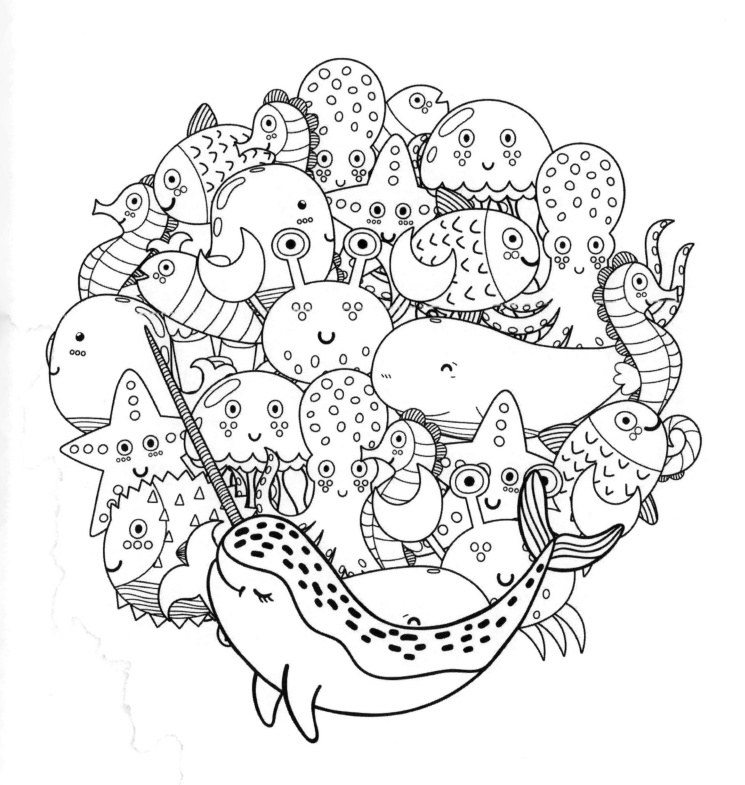

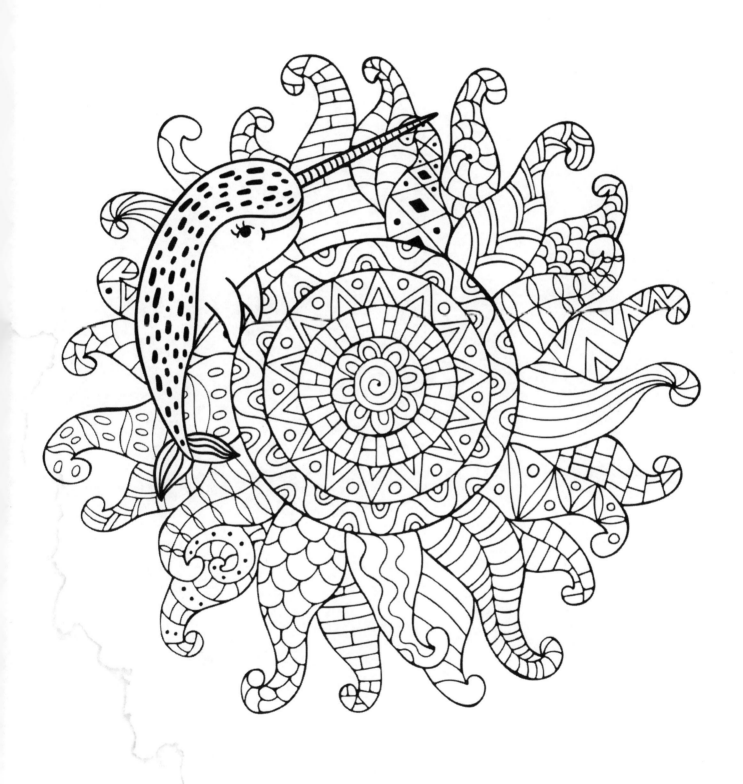

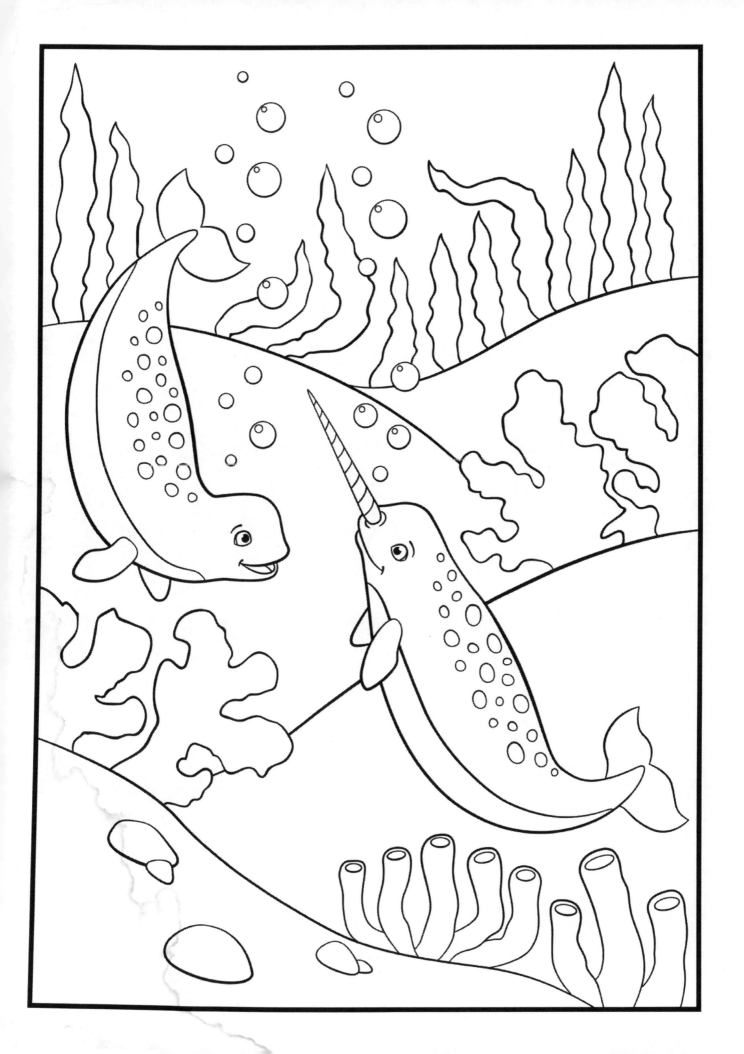

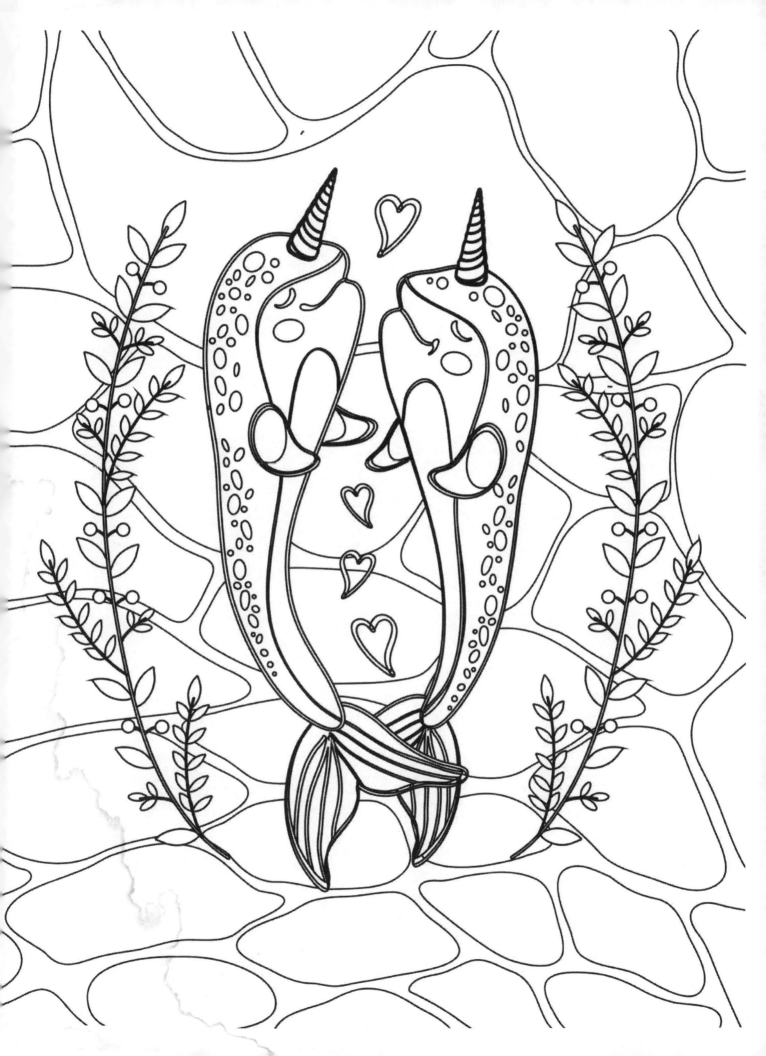

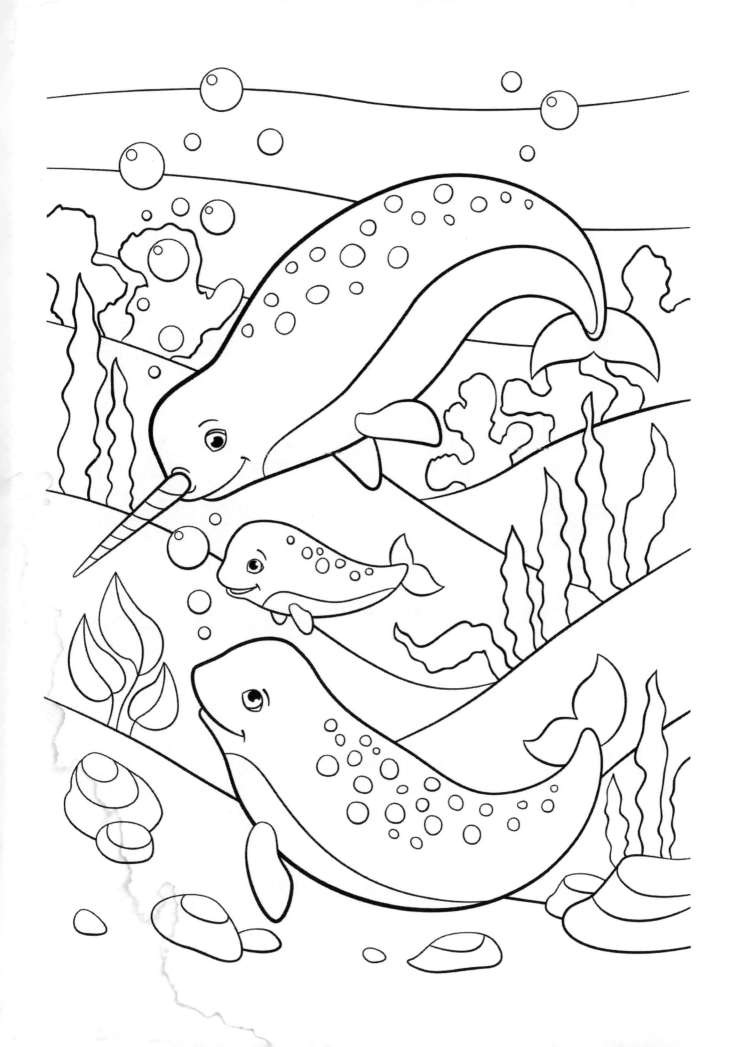

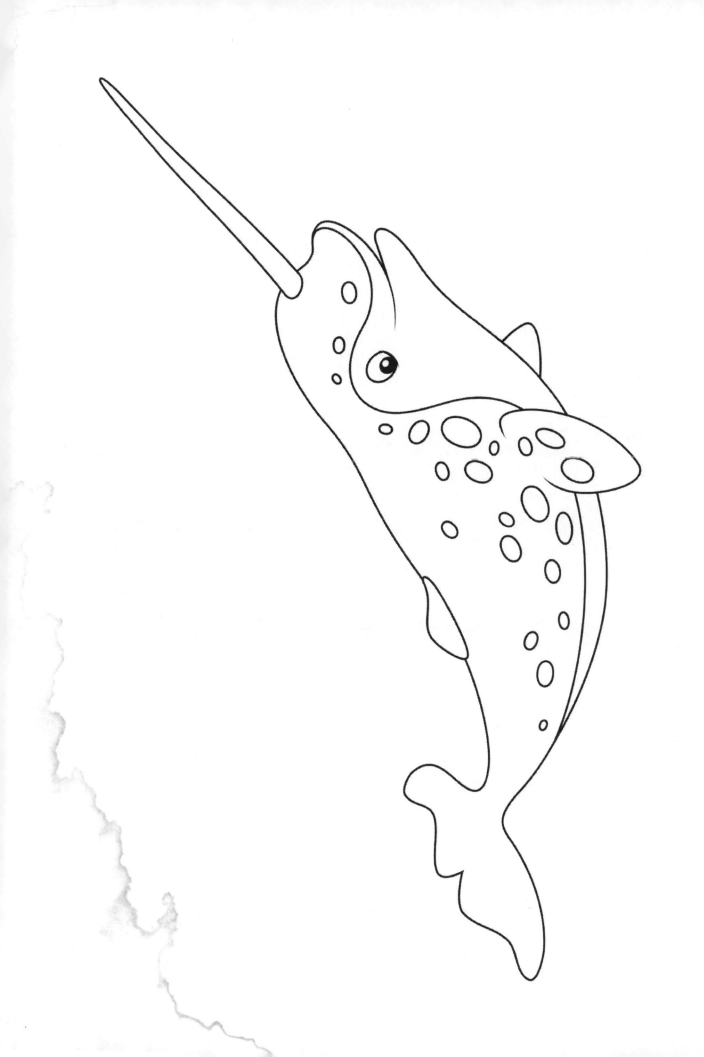

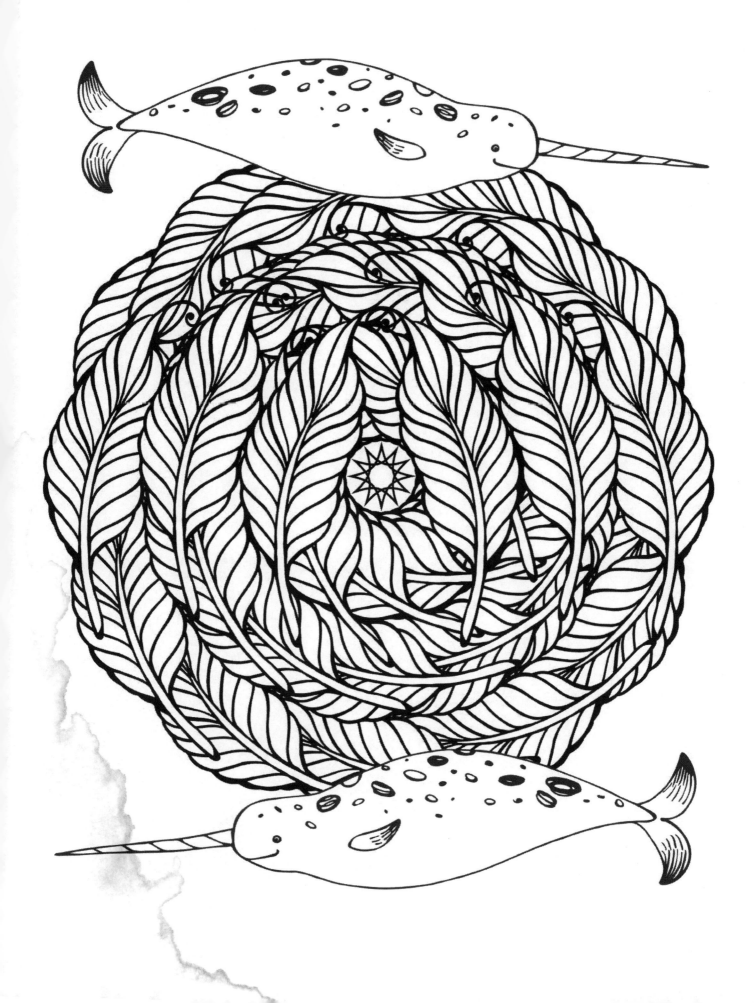

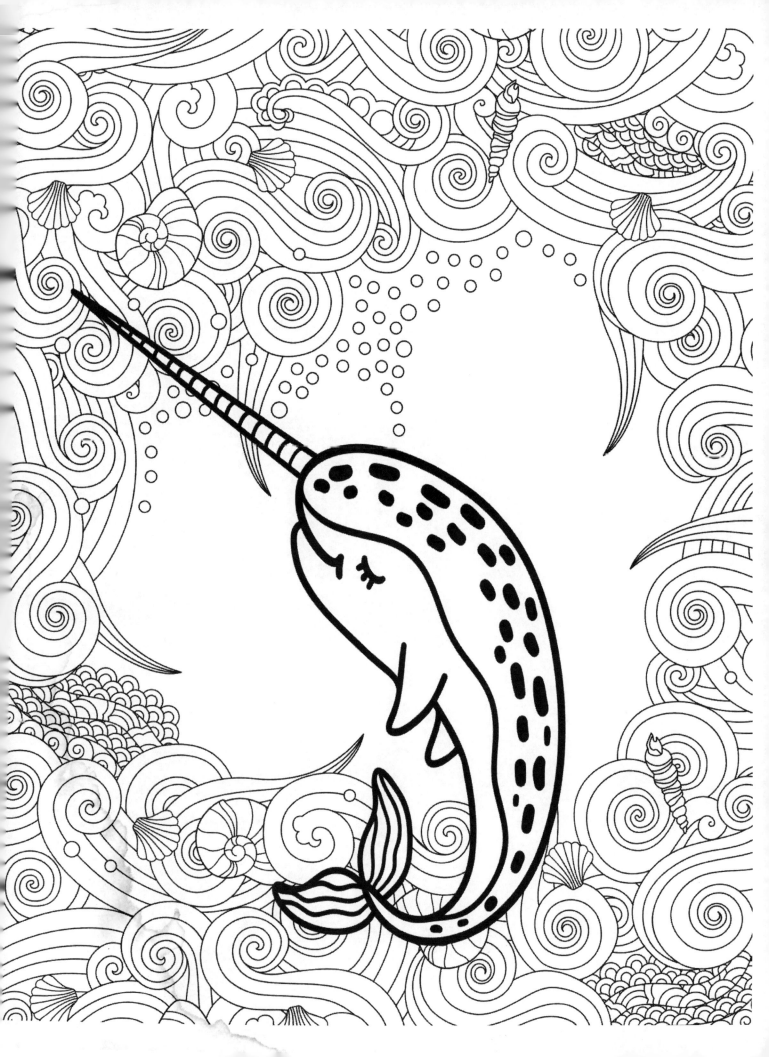

Enjoy this sweet moment

have A NICE day

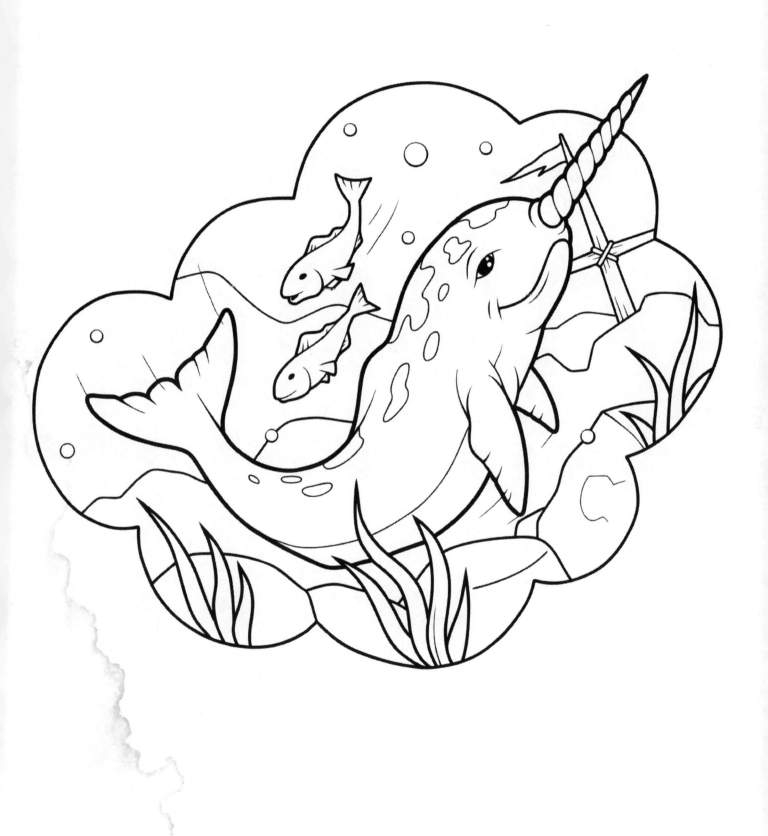

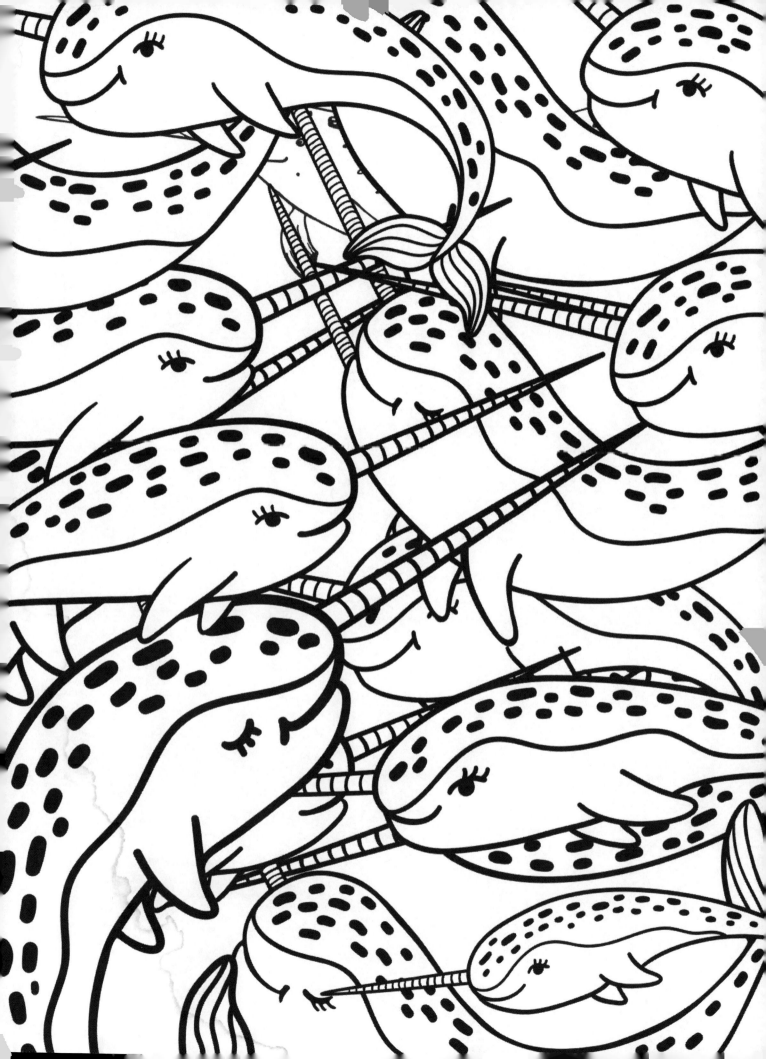

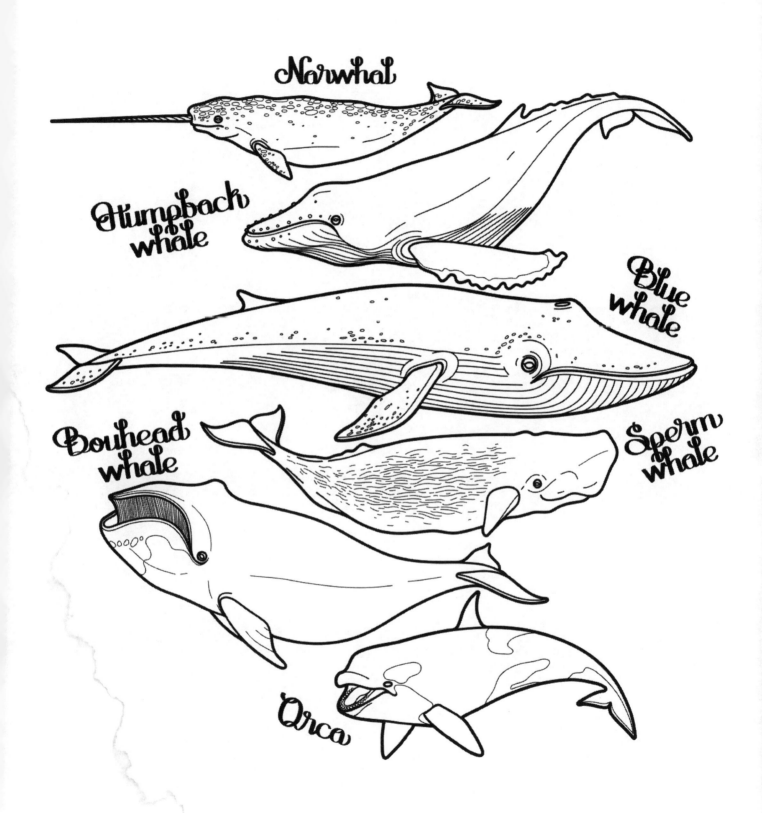

Narwhal

Humpback whale

Blue whale

Bowhead whale

Sperm whale

Orca

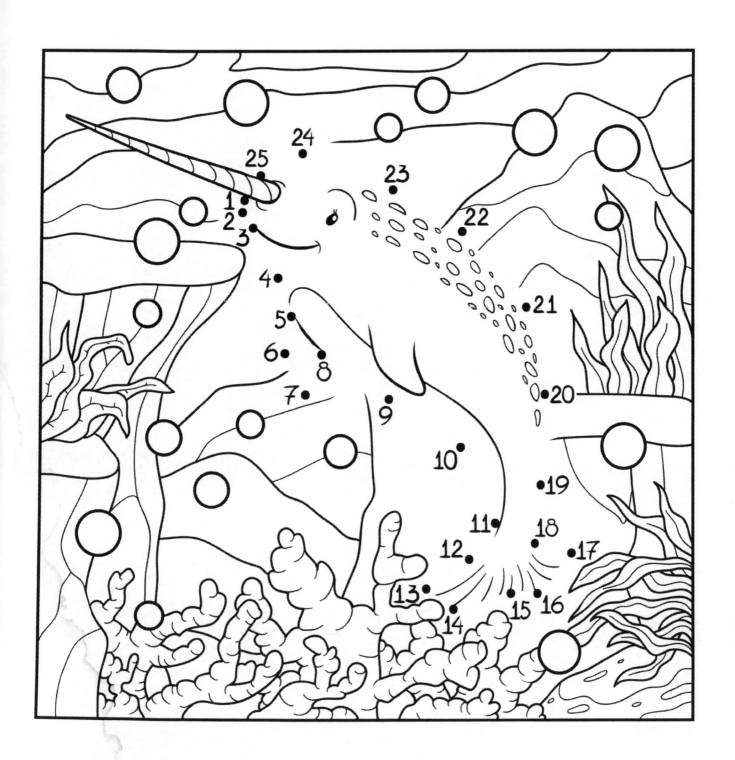

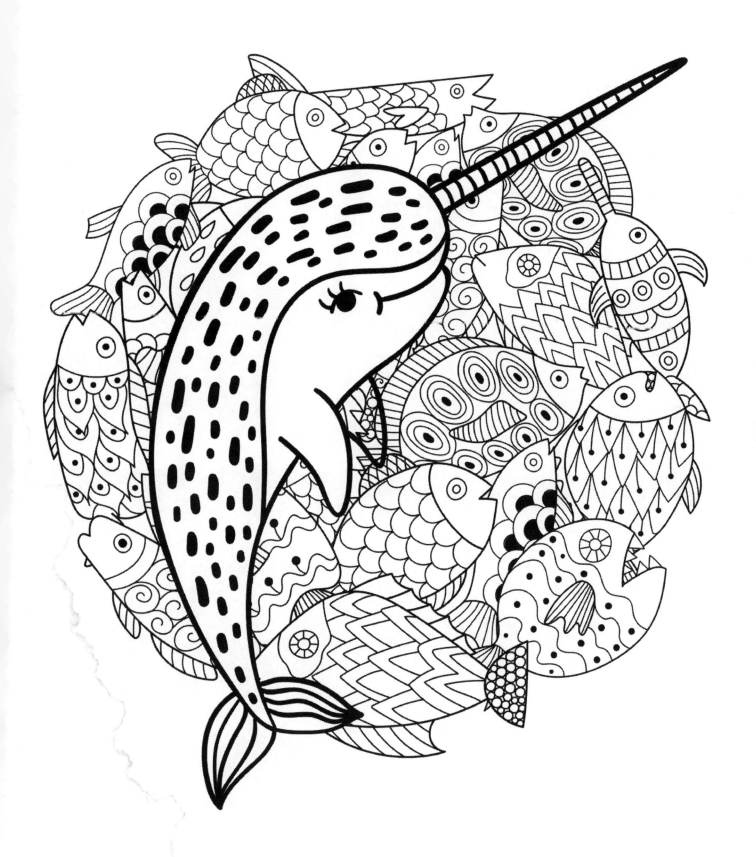

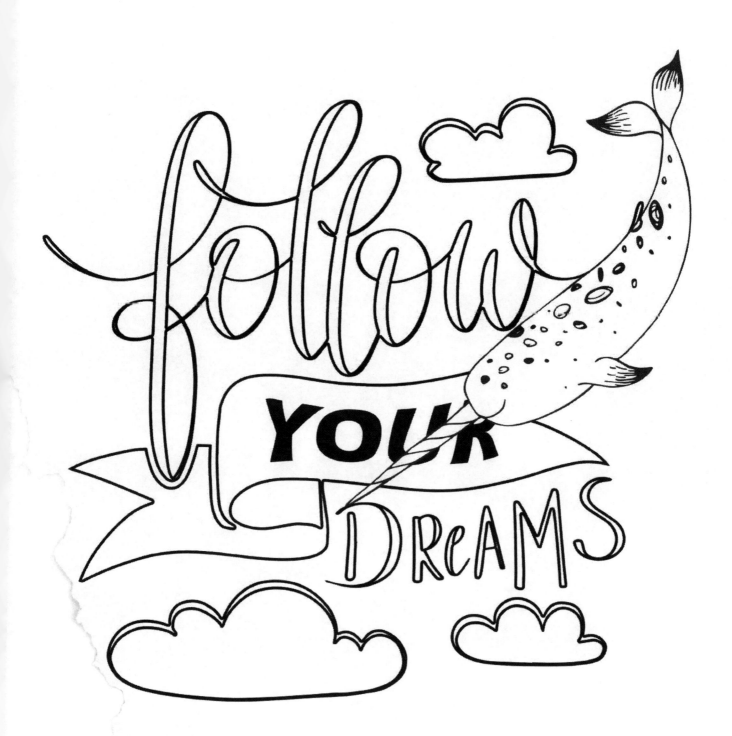

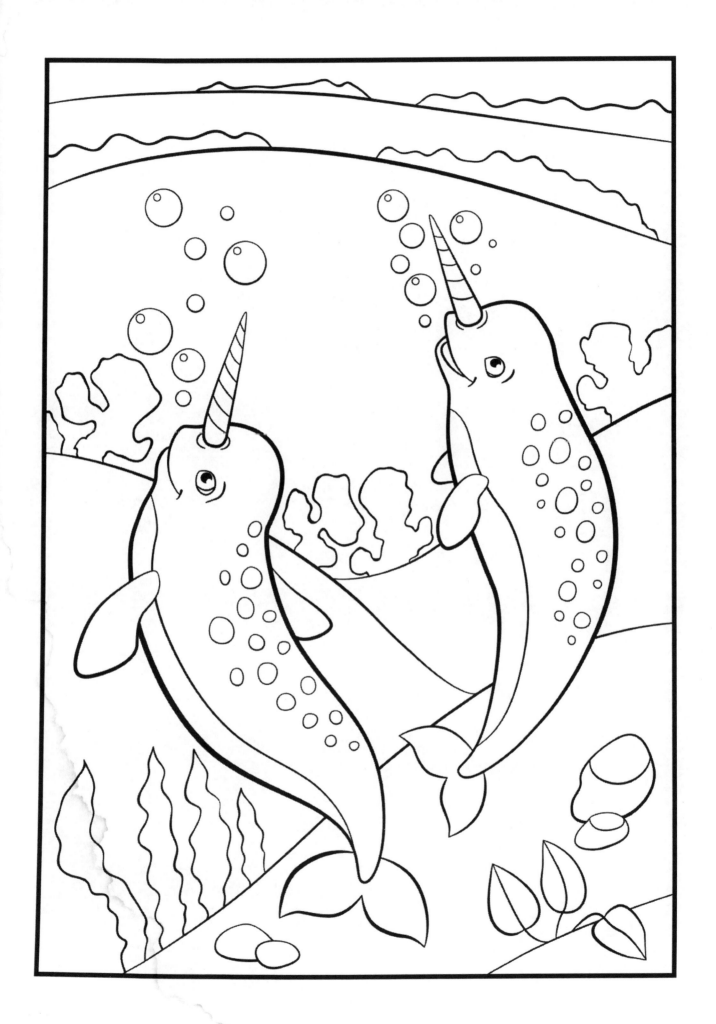

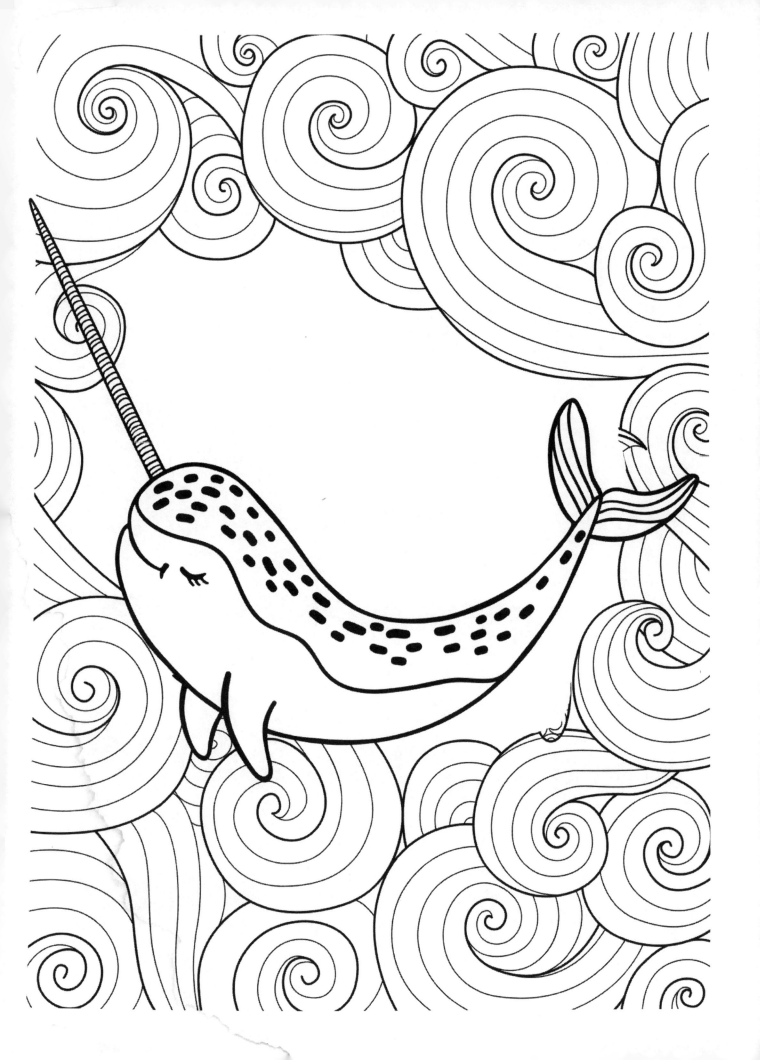

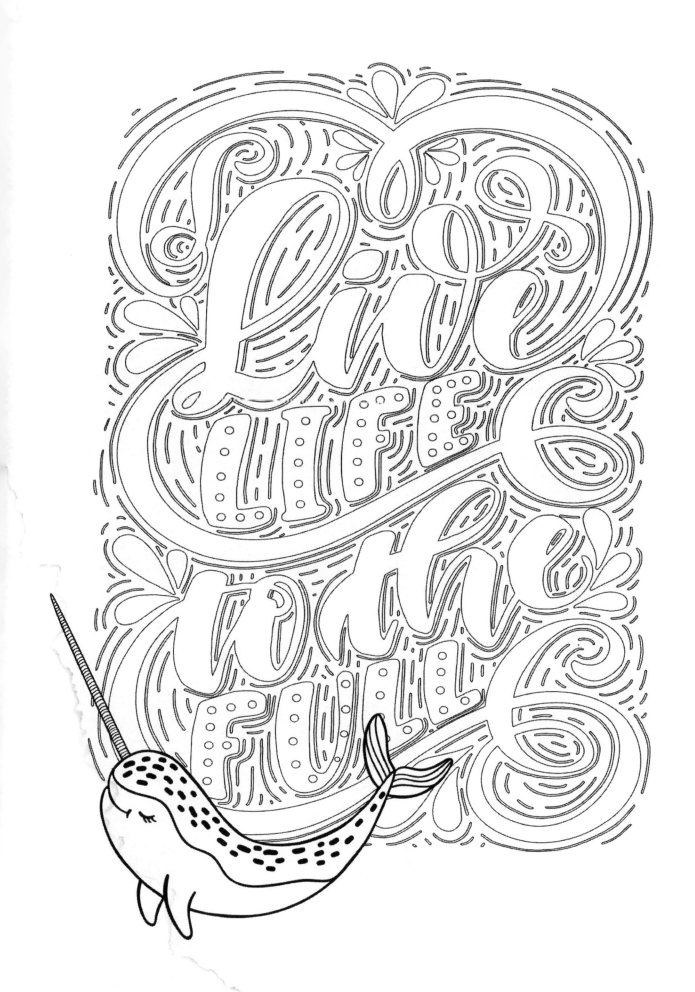

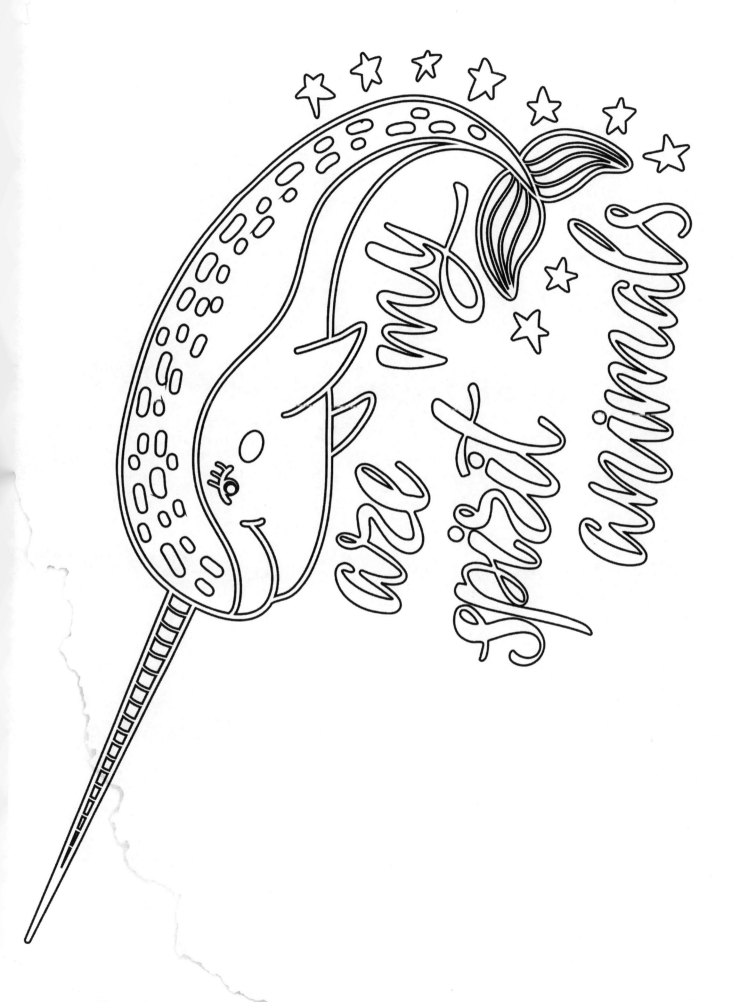

Made in the USA
Middletown, DE
01 December 2017